In the Year 1947

by

Kerry Butters.

In the Year 1947.

Millennium: 2nd millennium

Centuries: 19th century – **20th century** – 21st century

Decades: 1910s 1920s 1930s – **1940s** – 1950s 1960s 1970s

Years: 1944 1945 1946 – **1947** – 1948 1949 1950

1947 (MCMXLVII) was a common year starting on Wednesday (dominical letter E) of the Gregorian calendar, the 1947th year of the Common Era (CE) and *Anno Domini* (AD) designations, the 947th year of the 2nd millennium, the 47th year of the 20th century, and the 8th year of the 1940s decade.

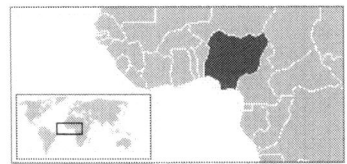

January 1: Nigeria gains autonomy.

Contents

- 1 Events
- 2 Births
- 3 Deaths
- 4 Nobel Prizes
- 5 In the News

Events

January

- January–February – Winter of 1946–47 in the United Kingdom: Worst snowfall in the country in the 20th century, with extensive disruption of travel. Given the low ratio of private vehicle ownership at the time this is mainly remembered in terms of the effects on the railway networks.
- January 1
    - British coal mines are nationalised.
    - Nigeria gains limited autonomy before gaining independence in 1960.
    - The Canadian Citizenship Act comes into effect.
- January 3 – Proceedings of the United States Congress are televised for the first time.
- January 10 – The United Nations takes control of the free city of Trieste.
- January 15 – Elizabeth Short, an aspiring actress nicknamed the "Black Dahlia", is found brutally murdered in a vacant lot in Los Angeles. The case remains unsolved to this day.
- January 16 – Vincent Auriol is inaugurated as president of France.

- January 19 – A shipwreck near Athens, Greece kills 392.
- January 24 – Dimitrios Maximos founds a monarchist government in Athens.
- January 25 – A Philippine plane crashes in Hong Kong, with $5 million worth of gold and money.
- January 25 – Famous gangster Al Capone dies.
- January 26 – A KLM Douglas C-47 Skytrain aircraft crashes soon after taking off from Kastrup Airport, Copenhagen, killing all on board, including Prince Gustaf Adolf, second in line to the Swedish throne, and the American singer Grace Moore.
- January 30 – February 8 – A heavy blizzard in Canada buries towns from Winnipeg, to Calgary.
- January 31 – The Communists take power in Poland.

February

- February 3
    - The lowest air temperature in North America (-63 degrees Celsius) is recorded in Snag in the Yukon Territory.
    - Percival Prattis becomes the first African-American news correspondent allowed in the United States House of Representatives and Senate press galleries.
- February 5
    - Bolesław Bierut becomes the President of Poland.
    - The Government of the United Kingdom announces the £25 million Tanganyika groundnut scheme for cultivation of peanuts in the Tanganyika Territory.
- February 6 – South Pacific Commission (SPC) founded.
- February 8 – Karlslust dance hall fire in Berlin, Germany, kills over 80 people.

- February 10 – In Paris, France, peace treaties are signed between the World War II Allies and Italy, Hungary, Romania, Bulgaria, and Finland. Italy cedes most of Istria to the Socialist Federal Republic of Yugoslavia (later Croatia).
- February 12
    - A meteor creates an impact crater in Sikhote-Alin, in the Soviet Union.
    - Christian Dior introduces The "New Look" in women's fashion, in Paris.
    - In Burma, the Panglong Agreement is reached between the Burmese government under its leader, General Aung San, and the Shan, Kachin, and Chin ethnic peoples at the Panglong Conference. U Aung Zan Wai, Pe Khin, Major Aung, Sir Maung Gyi, Dr. Sein Mya Maung and Myoma U Than Kywe are among the negotiators.
- February 17 – Cold War: The *Voice of America* begins to transmit radio broadcasts into Eastern Europe and the Soviet Union.
- February 20
    - An explosion at the O'Connor Electro-Plating Company in Los Angeles, leaves 17 dead, 100 buildings damaged, and a 22-foot-deep (6.7 m) crater in the ground.
    - U.S. Army Ordnance Corps Hermes program V-2 rocket *Blossom I* launched into space carrying plant material and fruitflies, the first animals to enter space.
- February 21 – In New York City, Edwin Land demonstrates the first "instant camera", his Polaroid Land Camera, to a meeting of the Optical Society of America.
- February 22 – *Tom and Jerry* cartoon *Cat Fishin'*, is released.

- February 23 – The International Organization for Standardization (ISO) is founded.
- February 25
    - The German state of Prussia is officially abolished by the Allied Control Council.
    - The worst-ever train crash in Japan kills 184 people.
    - John C. Hennessy, Jr., brings the first Volkswagen Beetle to the United States. He purchased the 1946 automobile from the U.S. Army Post Exchange in Frankfurt, Germany, while serving in the U.S. Army. The Beetle was shipped from Bremerhaven, arriving in New York this day.
- February 28
    - The United States grants France a military base in Casablanca.
    - In Taiwan, civil disorder is put down with large loss of civilian lives.

March

- March 1
    - The International Monetary Fund begins to operate.
    - Wernher von Braun marries his first cousin, the 18-year-old Maria von Quirstorp.
- March 4 – Treaty of Dunkirk (coming into effect 8 September) signed between the United Kingdom and France providing for mutual assistance in the event of attack.
- March 9 – Carrie Chapman Catt dies in New Rochelle.
- March 12 – The Truman Doctrine is proclaimed to help stem the spread of Communism.

- March 14 – Thames flood and other widespread flooding as the exceptionally harsh British winter of 1946–1947 ends in a thaw.
- March 15 – Hindus and Muslims clash in Punjab.
- March 19 – The 19th Academy Awards ceremony is held. The movie *The Best Years of Our Lives* wins the Academy Award for Best Picture, along with several other Academy Awards.
- March 25 – A coal mine explosion in Centralia, Illinois, kills 111 miners.
- March 28 – A World War II Japanese booby trap explodes on Corregidor island, killing 28 people.
- March 29 – A rebellion against French rule erupts in Madagascar.
- March 31 – The leaders of the Kurdish People's Republic of Mahabad, the second Kurdish state in the history of Iran, are hanged at the Chuwarchira Square in Mahabad after that country had been overrun by the Iranian army.

April

- April – Previous discovery of the 'Dead Sea Scrolls' in the Qumran Caves (above the northwest shore of the Dead Sea) by Bedouin shepherds, becomes known.
- April 1
  - Jackie Robinson, the first African American in Major League Baseball since the 1880s, signs a contract with the Brooklyn Dodgers.
  - King George II of Greece is succeeded by his brother King Paul I.
- April 4 – International Civil Aviation Organization begins operations.

- April 7
  - Edaville Railroad was opened as the first railway theme parks.
  - The largest recorded sunspot group appears on the solar surface.
- April 9
  - Multiple tornadoes strike Texas, Oklahoma, and Kansas killing 181 and injuring 970.
  - the Journey of Reconciliation began, organized by the Congress of Racial Equality
- April 15 – Jackie Robinson becomes the first African American to play Major League Baseball since the 1880s.
- April 16
  - Texas City disaster: The ammonium nitrate cargo of French-registered Liberty ship SS *Grandcamp* explodes in Texas City, Texas, killing at least 581, including all but one member of the city fire department, injuring at least 5,000 and destroying 20 city blocks. Of the dead, remains of 113 are never found and 63 are unidentifiable.
  - American financier and presidential adviser Bernard Baruch describes the post–World War II tensions between the Soviet Union and the United States as a "Cold War".
- April 18
  - The British Royal Navy detonates 6,800 tons of explosives in an attempt to demolish the fortified island of Heligoland, Germany, thus creating one of the largest man-made non-nuclear explosions in history.
  - Mrs. Ples is discovered in the Sterkfontein area in Transvaal, South Africa.

- April 26 – Academy-Award winning *Tom and Jerry* cartoon, *The Cat Concerto*, is released to theatres.

May

- May 1 – Portella della Ginestra massacre: The Salvatore Giuliano gang of Sicilian separatists opens fire on a Labour Day parade at Portella della Ginestra, Sicily, killing 11 people and wounding 27.
- May 2 – The movie *Miracle on 34th Street*, a Christmastime classic, is first shown in theaters.
- May 3 – The new post-war Japanese constitution goes into effect.
- May 12 – The animated cartoon film *Rabbit Transit*, directed by Friz Freleng, is released.
- May 22
  - The Cold War begins: In an effort to fight the spread of Communism, President Harry S. Truman signs an Act of Congress that implements the Truman Doctrine. This Act grants $400 million in military and economic aid to Turkey and Greece. The Cold War ended in 1991.
  - David Lean's film *Great Expectations*, based on the novel by Charles Dickens, opens in the United States. Critics call it the finest film ever made from a Charles Dickens novel.
- May 25 – An airliner of the Flugfelag Íslands crashes into a mountainside, killing 25 people.
-

June

Marshall Plan.

- June – The Doomsday Clock of the Bulletin of the Atomic Scientists is introduced.
- June 5 – U.S. Secretary of State George Marshall outlines the Marshall Plan for American reconstruction and relief aid to Europe in a speech at Harvard University.
- June 7 – The Royal Romanian Army founds the Association football club FC Steaua București, which will become the most successful Romanian football team, as *A.S.A. București*.
- June 10 – SAAB in Sweden produces its first automobile.
- June 11–15 – First Llangollen International Musical Eisteddfod is held in Wales. June 15 – The Portuguese government orders 11 military officers and 19 university professors who are accused of revolutionary activity to resign.
- June 21
    - Seaman Harold Dahl claims to have seen six unidentified flying objects (UFOs) near Maury Island in Puget Sound, Washington. On the next morning, Dahl reports the first modern so-called "Men in Black" encounter.
    - The Canadian Parliament votes unanimously to pass several laws regarding displaced foreign refugees.
- June 23 – The United States Senate follows the House of Representatives in overriding President Harry S. Truman's veto of the Taft–Hartley Act.

- June 24 – Kenneth Arnold makes the first widely reported UFO sighting near Mount Rainier, Washington.
- June 25 – *The Diary of a Young Girl* by Anne Frank is published for the first time as *Het Achterhuis: Dagboekbrieven 14 juni 1942 – 1 augustus 1944* ("The Annex: Diary Notes from 14 June 1942 – 1 August 1944") in Amsterdam, two years after the writer's death in Bergen-Belsen concentration camp.

July

- July 6 – The AK-47 assault rifle enters production, becoming the most produced gun in history.
- July 8 – A supposedly downed extraterrestrial spacecraft is reportedly found in the Roswell UFO incident, near Roswell, New Mexico, which was written about by Stanton T. Friedman.
- July 10 – In the UK, Princess Elizabeth announces her engagement to Lieutenant Philip Mountbatten.
- July 11 – The *Exodus* leaves France for Palestine, with 4,500 Jewish Holocaust survivor refugees on board.
- July 17
  - The Indian passenger ship SS *Ramdas* is capsized by a cyclone at Mumbai, India, with 625 people killed.
  - This is the alleged date when Raoul Wallenberg dies in a Soviet prison. It is not announced until February 6, 1957. There will be reported sightings of him until 1987.
- July 18
  - Following wide media and UNSCOP coverage, the *Exodus* is captured by British troops and refused entry into Palestine at the port of Haifa.
  - President Harry S. Truman signs the Presidential Succession Act into law, which places the Speaker of

the House and the President pro tempore of the Senate next in the line of succession after the Vice President.
- July 19 – Burmese nationalist Aung San and six members of his newly formed cabinet are assassinated during a cabinet meeting.
- July 26 – Cold War: U.S. President Harry S. Truman signs the National Security Act of 1947 into law, creating the Central Intelligence Agency, the Department of Defense, the Joint Chiefs of Staff, and the National Security Council.
- July 27–28 – English endurance swimmer Tom Blower becomes the first person to swim the North Channel, from Donaghadee in Northern Ireland to Portpatrick in Scotland.
- July 29 – After being shut down on November 9, 1946, for a refurbishment, the ENIAC computer, the world's first electronic digital computer, is turned back on again. It next remains in continuous operation until October 2, 1955.

August

Flag of the newly independent India

- August 5 – The Netherlands stops all "police actions" in Indonesia.
- August 7
    - Thor Heyerdahl's balsa wood raft, the *Kon-Tiki*, smashes into the reef at Raroia in the Tuamotu Islands after a 101-day, 4,300 mile, voyage across the Eastern

Pacific Ocean, proving that pre-historic peoples could hypothetically have traveled to the Central Pacific islands from South America.
    - The Bombay Municipal Corporation formally takes over the Bombay Electric Supply and Transport (BEST).
- August 14
    - The Muslim majority region formed by the Partition of India gains independence from the British Empire and adopts the name **Pakistan**. While the transition is officially at midnight on this day, Pakistan celebrates its independence on August 14, compared with India on the 15th, because the Pakistan Standard Time is 30 minutes behind the standard time of India.
    - Muhammad Ali Jinnah becomes the first Governor-General of Pakistan. Liaquat Ali Khan takes office as the first Prime Minister of Pakistan
- August 15
    - The greater Indian subcontinent with a mixed population of Hindus, Muslims, Christians, Sikhs, Buddhists, Jains, Jews, etc. formed by the Partition of India gain independence from the British Empire and retains the name **India**.
    - Louis Mountbatten becomes the first Governor-General of India. Jawaharlal Nehru takes office as the first Prime Minister of India.
- August 16 – In Greece, General Markos Vafiadis takes over the government.
- August 23 – The Prime Minister of Greece, Dimitrios Maximos, resigns.
- August 27 – The French government lowers the daily bread ration to 200 grams, causing riots in Verdun and in Le Mans.

- August 30 – A fire at a movie theater in Rueil, a suburb of Paris, France kills 87 people.
- August 31 – The communists seize power in Hungary.

September

The Central Intelligence Agency (CIA), officially born September 18, 1947

- September 9 – A moth lodged in a relay is found to be the cause of a malfunction in the Harvard Mark II electromechanical computer, logged as "First actual case of bug being found."
- September 13 – Indian Prime Minister Jawaharlal Nehru suggests the exchange of four million Hindus and Muslims between India and Pakistan.
- September 17–September 21 – The 1947 Fort Lauderdale hurricane in southeastern Florida, and also in Alabama, Mississippi, and Louisiana causes widespread damage and kills 51 people.
- September 18
    - National Security Act of 1947 becomes effective on this day creating the United States Air Force, National Security Council and the Central Intelligence Agency.

- ○ War Department becomes the Department of the Army, a branch of the new Department of Defense.
- September 22 – Information Bureau of the Communist and Workers' Parties (Communist Information Bureau) ("Cominform") is founded.
- September 30 – Pakistan and Yemen join the United Nations.

October

- October – First recorded use of the word *computer* in its modern sense, referring to an electronic digital machine.
- October 5 – President Harry S. Truman delivers the first televised White House address speaking on the world food crises.
- October 14 – The United States Air Force test pilot, Captain Chuck Yeager, flies a Bell X-1 rocket plane faster than the speed of sound, the first time it has been accomplished
- October 20 – A war begins in Kashmir, along the border between India and Pakistan, leading to the Indo-Pakistani War of 1947 in the following year. Also, Pakistan established diplomatic relations with the United States of America.
- October 24 – The first Azad Kashmir Government is established within Pakistan, headed by Sardar Muhammad Ibrahim Khan as its first President supported by the government of Pakistan.
- October 30 – The General Agreement on Tariffs and Trade (GATT), the foundation of the World Trade Organization (WTO), is established.
-

November

- November 2
  - In Long Beach, California, the designer and airplane pilot Howard Hughes carries out the one and only flight of the *Hughes H-4 Hercules*, the largest fixed-wing aircraft ever built and flown. This flight only lasted eight minutes.
  - An earthquake in the Chilean Andes kills 233 people.
- November 6 – The program *Meet the Press* makes its television debut on the NBC-TV network in the United States.
- November 9 – Junagadh is invaded by the Indian army.
- November 10 – The arrest of four steel workers in Marseille begins a French communist riot that also spreads to Paris.
- November 15
  - International Telecommunication Union becomes a specialized agency of the United Nations.
  - Universal Postal Union (UPU) becomes a specialized agency of the United Nations (effective 1 July 1948).
- November 16
  - In Brussels, 15,000 people demonstrate against the relatively short prison sentences of Belgian Nazi criminals.
  - Great Britain began withdrawing its troops from Palestine.
- November 18 – The Ballantyne's Department Store fire in Christchurch, New Zealand, kills 41 people.

- November 20
    - The Princess Elizabeth (later Elizabeth II), the daughter of George VI, marries The Duke of Edinburgh at Westminster Abbey in London, United Kingdom.
    - Paul Ramadier resigns as the Prime Minister of France. He is succeeded by Robert Schuman, who calls 80,000 army reservists to quell rioting miners in France.
- November 21 – The United Nations Conference on Trade and Employment begins in Havana, Cuba. This conference ends in 1948, when its members finish the Havana Charter.
- November 24 – McCarthyism: The United States House of Representatives votes 346–17 to approve citations of Contempt of Congress against the "Hollywood Ten" after the screenwriters and directors refuse to co-operate with the House Un-American Activities Committee concerning allegations of communist influences in the movie business. The ten men are blacklisted by the Hollywood movie studios on the following day.
- November 25
    - The Parliament of New Zealand ratifies the Statute of Westminster, and thus becomes independent of legislative control by the Parliament of the United Kingdom.
    - The new Pakistan Army and Pashtun mercenaries overrun Mirpur in Kashmir, resulting in the death of 20,000 Hindus and Sikhs.
- November 27 – In Paris, France, police occupy the editorial offices of the communist newspapers.
- November 29 – The United Nations General Assembly votes to partition Palestine between Arab and Jewish regions, which results in the creation of the State of Israel.

December

- December 3
    - French communist strikers derail the Paris-Tourcoing express train because of false rumors that it was transporting soldiers. 21 people are killed.
    - The Tennessee Williams play *A Streetcar Named Desire*, starring Marlon Brando in his first great role, opens at the Ethel Barrymore Theatre on Broadway. Jessica Tandy also stars as Blanche Du Bois.
- December 4 – The French Interior Minister, Jules S. Moch, takes emergency measures against his country's rioters after six days of violent arguments in the National Assembly.
- December 6
    - Arturo Toscanini conducts a concert performance of the first half of Giuseppe Verdi's opera *Otello* for a broadcast on NBC Radio in the United States. The second half of the opera is broadcast a week later.
    - Women are admitted to full membership of the University of Cambridge in England following a vote in September.
- December 9 – French labor unions call off the general strike and re-commence negotiations with the French government.
- December 12 – The Iranian Royal Army takes back power in the Azerbaijan province.
- December 21 – 400,000 slaughtered during mass migration of Hindus and Muslims into the new states India and Pakistan.
- December 22
    - The Italian Constituent Assembly votes to accept the new Constitution of Italy.

- o The first practical electronic transistor is demonstrated by Bardeen, Brattain, and Shockley of the United States.
- December 30 – King Michael I of Romania abdicates.

Date unknown

- The House Un-American Activities Committee begins its investigations into communism in Hollywood.
- Mikhail Kalashnikov's AK-47 assault rifle is accepted as the standard small arm of the Soviet military.
- Raytheon produces the first commercial microwave oven.
- Women's suffrage is granted in Argentina.
- The longest ever Ice cream serving career, the one of Allen Gans, started in 1947 in Boston.

In fiction

- The song "Sgt. Pepper's Lonely Hearts Club Band" mentions Sgt. Pepper teaching the band to play "20 years ago today". This would place the event somewhere between February 1 and June 1 of 1947.
- *L.A. Noire*, a video game released in 2011 by Rockstar Games, takes place in Los Angeles throughout the year 1947.

Births

January

David Bowie

Andrea Martin

- January 1
    - F. R. David, Tunisian-born French singer
    - Leon Patillo, American Christian musician
    - Vladimir Titov, Russian cosmonaut
    - Frances Yip, Hong Kong singer
- January 2 – Jack Hanna, American zoologist
- January 4 – Chris Cutler, English percussionist
- January 5 – Mercury Morris, American football player
- January 6 – Sandy Denny, British singer (d. 1978)
- January 7 – Shobhaa De, Indian writer
- January 8
    - David Bowie, English singer-songwriter (d. 2016)
    - Samuel Schmid, Swiss Federal Councilor
    - Terry Sylvester, English singer and musician

- o Laurie Walters, American actress
- January 9
  - o Nic Jones, English folk singer
  - o Ronnie Landfield, American artist
- January 10 – Peer Steinbrück, German politician
- January 11 – Mart Smeets, Dutch sports journalist
- January 14 – Bill Werbeniuk, Canadian snooker player (d. 2003)
- January 15 –
  - o Andrea Martin, American actress
  - o Michael Schanze, German television presenter
- January 16
  - o Apasra Hongsakula, Miss Universe 1965
  - o Laura Schlessinger, American radio and TV talk show host
- January 18 – Takeshi Kitano, Japanese film director and actor
- January 19 – Paula Deen, Food Channel star
- January 21 – Jill Eikenberry, American actress
- January 23
  - o Thomas R. Carper, U.S. Senator from Delaware
  - o Megawati Sukarnoputri, former President of Indonesia
- January 24
  - o Michio Kaku, American theoretical physicist
  - o Masashi Ozaki, Japanese golfer
  - o Warren Zevon, American rock musician (d. 2003)
- January 25 – Eduardo Gonçalves de Andrade (Tostão), Brazilian football player
- January 27
  - o Björn Afzelius, Swedish singer-songwriter and guitarist (Hoola Bandoola Band) (d. 1999)
  - o Vyron Polydoras, Greek politician

- Cal Schenkel, American illustrator
- Philip Sugden, English historian (d. 2014)
- January 29 – Linda B. Buck, American biologist, recipient of the Nobel Prize in Physiology or Medicine
- January 30
  - Ileana Jacket, German born-Venezuelan actress.
  - Steve Marriott, British rock musician (d. 1991)
- January 31 – Nolan Ryan, American baseball player

February

Farrah Fawcett

Dan Quayle

- February 1 – Jessica Savitch, American journalist (d. 1983)
- February 2 – Farrah Fawcett, American actress (d. 2009)
- February 3
  - Paul Auster, American novelist
  - Melanie Safka, American rock singer
  -

- February 4
    - Dennis C. Blair, American admiral and Director of National Intelligence
    - Dan Quayle, 44th Vice President of the United States
- February 5 – Darrell Waltrip, American race car driver and broadcaster
- February 7 – Wayne Allwine, American voice actor (d. 2009)
- February 10
    - Louise Arbour, Canadian jurist
    - Nicholas Owen, English newsreader (ITN)
- February 11
    - Yukio Hatoyama, 60th Prime Minister of Japan
    - Derek Shulman, Lead Singer of Gentle Giant
- February 12 – Jarnail Singh Bhindranwale, Punjabi saint, Sikh theologian, military leader (d. 1984)
- February 13 – Mike Krzyzewski, American basketball coach
- February 15
    - John Adams, American composer
    - Wenche Myhre, Norwegian actress and singer
    - Ádám Nádasdy, Hungarian linguist and poet
- February 18
    - Princess Christina of the Netherlands
    - Dennis DeYoung, American rock musician (Styx)
- February 19 – Gustavo Rodríguez, Venezuelan actor (d. 2014)
- February 20
    - Peter Osgood, English footballer (d. 2006)
    - Peter Strauss, American actor
- February 21 – Victor Sokolov, Russian dissident journalist and priest (d. 2006)
-

- February 24
    - Rupert Holmes, British-born American singer-songwriter
    - Edward James Olmos, American actor (*Stand and Deliver*)
- February 25 – Doug Yule, American rock singer and musician (The Velvet Underground)
- February 26 – Sandie Shaw, British singer
- February 27 – Gidon Kremer, Latvian violinist
- February 28 – Stephanie Beacham, English actress

March

Alan Thicke

Dick Fosbury

Glenn Close

Elton John

- March 1 – Alan Thicke, Canadian actor and television host
- March 4
    - David Franzoni, American screenwriter
    - Jan Garbarek, Norwegian musician
    - Gunnar Hansen, Icelandic actor (d. 2015)
- March 6
    - Kiki Dee, English pop singer
    - Dick Fosbury, American athlete
    - Teru Miyamoto, Japanese author
    - Rob Reiner, American actor, comedian, producer, director, activist
- March 7 – Walter Röhrl, German race car driver
- March 8
    - Carole Bayer Sager, American singer-songwriter

- Michael S. Hart, American author and inventor (d. 2011)
- March 10
  - Kim Campbell, 19th Prime Minister of Canada
  - Tom Scholz, American musician, songwriter and inventor
- March 11
  - David Ferguson, American music producer and activist
  - Geoff Hunt, Australian squash player
- March 12
  - Kalervo Palsa, a Finnish artist
  - Mitt Romney, American businessman, politician, former Governor of Massachusetts and 2012 presidential candidate
- March 13 – Beat Richner, Swiss pediatrician and cellist
- March 14 – Pam Ayres, British poet
- March 15 – Ry Cooder, American guitarist
- March 16
  - Baek Yoon-sik, South Korean actor
  - Ramzan Paskayev, Chechen accordionist
- March 17 – Yury Chernavsky, Russian-born composer and producer
- March 18 – Tamara Griesser Pečar, Slovenian historian
- March 19 – Glenn Close, American actress
- March 20 – John Boswell, American historian (d. 1994)
- March 22 – James Patterson, American author
  - Florence Warner, Voice of Adult Abigail the Woman in Once Upon a Forest
- March 24
  - Louise Lanctôt, Canadian terrorist and writer
  - Alan Sugar, Baron Sugar, English entrepreneur

- March 25 – Elton John, English rock singer, pianist and songwriter
- March 27 – Walt Mossberg, American newspaper columnist

April

Gloria Macapagal-Arroyo

David Letterman

James Woods

Iggy Pop

Johan Cruijff

John Ratzenberger

- April 1
    - Alain Connes, French mathematician
    - Ingrid Steeger, German actress and comedian
- April 2
    - Emmylou Harris, American singer-songwriter
    - Camille Paglia, American literary critic
- April 4 – Eliseo Soriano, Philippine preacher
- April 5 – Gloria Macapagal-Arroyo, former Philippine president and daughter of former president Diosdado Macapagal
- April 6 – John Ratzenberger, American actor
- April 8
    - Tom DeLay, American politician
    - Robert Kiyosaki, American investor, businessman, self-help author
- April 11 – Meshach Taylor, American actor (d. 2014)

- April 12
    - Tom Clancy, American author (d. 2013)
    - David Letterman, American talk show host
- April 15
    - Mike Chapman, Australian-born songwriter, record producer
    - Lois Chiles, American actress
    - Roy Raymond (businessman), American entrepreneur and founder of Victoria's Secret (d. 1993)
- April 16
    - Kareem Abdul-Jabbar, American pro basketball player
    - Gerry Rafferty, Scottish singer-songwriter (d. 2011)
- April 17 – Jerzy Stuhr, Polish actor and director
- April 18
    - Kathy Acker, American author (d. 1997)
    - James Woods, American actor
- April 19 – Murray Perahia, American pianist
- April 20 – Hector, Finnish rock musician
- April 20 – Anwar Ibrahim, Malaysian politician
- April 21 – Iggy Pop, American rock musician
- April 25 – Johan Cruijff, Dutch footballer and coach (d. 2016)
- April 28 – Ken St. Andre, American game designer and author
- April 29 – Tommy James, American rock singer and producer
- April 30 – Leslie Grantham, English actor

May

Richard Jenkins

Ken Westerfield

- May 4
  - Richard Jenkins, American actor
  - Theda Skocpol, American sociologist
- May 6 – Martha Nussbaum, American philosopher
- May 8 – H. Robert Horvitz, American biologist, recipient of the Nobel Prize in Physiology or Medicine
- May 11 – Walter Selke, German physicist
- May 12 – Michael Ignatieff, Canadian politician, philosopher and historian
- May 13 – Stephen R. Donaldson, American novelist
- May 19 – Paul Brady, Northern Irish singer/songwriter
- May 23 – Ken Westerfield, Disc sports (Frisbee) pioneer, athlete, showman, promoter
- May 24 – Maude Barlow, Canadian author, activist and National Chairperson of The Council of Canadians
- May 26 – Glenn Turner, New Zealand cricket captain
-

- May 27
  - Branko Oblak, Slovenian football player and coach
  - Peter DeFazio, American politician
- May 29 – Stan Zemanek, Australian radio broadcaster (d. 2007)

June

- June 1
  - Jonathan Pryce, Welsh actor
  - Ronnie Wood, English rock musician (The Faces, The Rolling Stones)
- June 4 – Viktor Klima, Chancellor of Austria
- June 5 – Laurie Anderson, American experimental performance artist, composer and musician
- June 5 – Jojon, Indonesian comedian and actor (d. 2014)
- June 6
  - David Blunkett, British politician
  - Robert Englund, American actor (*A Nightmare on Elm Street*)
  - Ada Kok, Dutch swimmer
- June 7 – Thurman Munson, American baseball catcher (d. 1979)
- June 8 – Eric F. Wieschaus, American biologist, recipient of the Nobel Prize in Physiology or Medicine
- June 14 – Barry Melton, American rock musician (Country Joe and the Fish)
- June 15 – John Hoagland, American war photographer (d. 1984)
- June 16 – -minu, Swiss columnist and writer
- June 19
  - Paula Koivuniemi, Finnish singer

- Salman Rushdie, Indian-born British author (*The Satanic Verses*)
- June 20 – Candy Clark, American actress
- June 21
  - Meredith Baxter, American actress
  - Shirin Ebadi, Iranian activist, recipient of the Nobel Peace Prize
  - Michael Gross, American actor
  - Fernando Savater, Spanish philosopher and author
- June 22
  - Octavia E. Butler, American author (d. 2006)
  - David Lander, American actor
  - Pete Maravich, American basketball player (d. 1988)
  - Jerry John Rawlings, former President of Ghana
- June 23 – Bryan Brown, Australian actor
- June 25 – Jimmie Walker, American actor
- June 28 – Mark Helprin, American writer
- June 29 – David Chiang, Hong Kong actor

July

Larry David

O. J. Simpson

Camilla, Duchess of Cornwall

Albert Brooks

Arnold Schwarzenegger

- July 2 – Larry David, American actor, writer, producer and director
- July 3
  - Dave Barry, American writer
  - Betty Buckley, American actress and singer
- July 5
  - Joe Brown (judge), TV Judge
- July 6 – Larnelle Harris, American Christian musician
- July 7
  - Richard Beckinsale, English actor (d. 1979)
  - Felix Standaert, Belgian diplomat
- July 8 – Bobby Sowell, American pianist and composer
- July 9
  - Haruomi Hosono, Japanese musician (Yellow Magic Orchestra)
  - Mitch Mitchell, English rock drummer (d. 2008)
  - O. J. Simpson, American football player, actor
- July 10 – Arlo Guthrie, American folk singer
- July 12 – Loren Coleman, American cryptozoologist and author
- July 17 – Camilla, Duchess of Cornwall, British Princess and second wife of Charles, Prince of Wales
- July 18 – Steven W. Mahoney, Canadian politician
- July 19
  - Bernie Leadon, American musician and songwriter
  - Brian May, English rock guitarist (Queen)
- July 20
  - Gerd Binnig, German physicist, Nobel Prize laureate
  - Carlos Santana, Mexican-born rock guitarist
- July 21 – Co Adriaanse, Dutch football manager
-

- July 22
  - Albert Brooks, American actor, comedian and director
  - Don Henley, American singer-songwriter and musician
- July 23 – Spencer Christian, American television personality
- July 24 – Peter Serkin, American pianist
- July 27
  - Bob Klein, American football player
  - Kazuyoshi Miura, Japanese businessman (d. 2008)
- July 30
  - William Atherton, American actor
  - Arnold Schwarzenegger, Austrian-born American actor, bodybuilder and 38th Governor of California
- July 31
  - Richard Griffiths, English actor (d. 2013)
  - Joe Wilson, American politician

August

- August 1 – Lorna Goodison, Jamaican poet
- August 3 – Colleen Corby, American fashion model
- August 4 – Hubert Ingraham, Bahamian politician
- August 6 – Mohammad Najibullah, former President of Afghanistan (d. 1996)
- August 7 – Franciscus Henri, Dutch-born Australian children's entertainer, composer and artist
- August 8 – Terangi Adam, Nauruan politician
- August 9 – John Varley, American science-fiction author
- August 10
  - Ian Anderson, British rock musician
  - Drupi, Italian singer
  - Anwar Ibrahim, Malaysian politician

- August 11 – Diether Krebs, German actor, cabaret artist and comedian. (d. 2000)
- August 12 – William Hartston, British chess player
- August 13 – John Stocker, Canadian voice actor
- August 14
    - Maddy Prior, English folk singer
    - Danielle Steel, American romance novelist
- August 15 – Raakhee, Indian actress
- August 16 – Marc Messier, Canadian actor
- August 19
    - Terry Hoeppner, American football coach (d. 2007)
    - Gerard Schwarz, American conductor
- August 22 – Cindy Williams, American actress
- August 23 – Willy Russell, British playwright
- August 24 – Roger De Vlaeminck, Belgian cyclist
- August 26 – Emiliano Díez, Cuban actor
- August 27 – Barbara Bach, American actress
- August 28 – Liza Wang, Hong Kong actress, Otis Surratt
- August 29
    - George Costigan, British actor and screenwriter
    - Temple Grandin, American animal welfare and autism expert
- August 30 – Allan Rock, Canadian politician and diplomat
- August 31
    - Ramón Castellano de Torres, Spanish painter
    - Somchai Wongsawat, Thai 26th Prime Minister

September

Sam Neill

Stephen King

Meat Loaf

- September 1 – Al Green, American politician
- September 3 – Kjell Magne Bondevik, Prime Minister of Norway
- September 5 – Kiyoshi Takayama, Japanese yakuza boss
- September 6
    - Jane Curtin, American actress and comedian

- Bruce Rioch, Scottish footballer and coach
- Jacob Rubinovitz, Israeli scientist.
- September 8 – Benjamin Orr, American singer-songwriter (d. 2000)
- September 9 – Freddy Weller, American singer-songwriter
- September 14 – Sam Neill, Northern Ireland-born New Zealand actor
- September 16 – Russ Abbot, British comedian and actor
- September 17 – Dame Tessa Jowell, British politician
- September 19
  - Steve Bartlett, American businessman, lobbyist, politician (former U.S. congressman from Texas's 3rd congressional district; former mayor of Dallas, Texas; member of the Dallas City Council)
  - Tanith Lee, British author (d. 2015)
- September 21
  - Don Felder, American musician and songwriter
  - Stephen King, American writer and novelist, specializing in the horror genre
- September 22
  - Jo Beverley, Anglo-Canadian writer (d. 2016)
  - Norma McCorvey, American abortion plaintiff (*Roe v. Wade*)
- September 23 – Mary Kay Place, American actress
- September 25
  - Ali Parvin, an Iranian footballer and coach
  - Cheryl Tiegs, American model and actress
- September 26 – Lynn Anderson, American country-music singer (d. 2015)
- September 27
  - Dick Advocaat, a Dutch football manager

- ○ Meat Loaf, American rock singer, actor
- September 28 – Sheikh Hasina, the Prime Minister of Bangladesh (1996–2001; 2009–present)
- September 30
  - ○ Marc Bolan, English rock musician (d. 1977)
  - ○ Rula Lenska, English actress

October

Brian Johnson

Kevin Kline

Hillary Clinton

Herman Van Rompuy

- October 1
    - Aaron Ciechanover, an Israeli biologist, winner of the Nobel Prize in Chemistry
    - Stephen Collins, American actor
- October 2 – Ward Churchill, American author and activist
- October 3 – Alain Mucchielli, French physician
    - Fred DeLuca, American entrepreneur and Co-founder of Subway (d. 2015)
- October 4 – Ann Widdecombe, British politician
- October 5 – Brian Johnson, English rock singer (AC/DC)
- October 6 – Gail Farrell, American singer
- October 7 – Pip Williams, British record producer
- October 8 – Stephen Shore, American photographer
- October 9 – France Gall, French singer
- October 10 – Larry Lamb, British actor
- October 13 – Sammy Hagar, American rock singer
- October 14 – Nikolai Volkoff, Croatian-Russian professional wrestler
- October 16 – Bob Weir, American rock guitarist
- October 17
    - Gene Green, American politician
    - Michael McKean, American actor and comedian

- October 18 – James H. Fallon, American neuroscientist
  - Job Cohen – Dutch politician
- October 19 – Giorgio Cavazzano, Italian comics artist and illustrator
  - October 19 – Gunnar Staalesen, Norwegian author
- October 22 – Ed Welch, English TV-music composer
- October 24 – Kevin Kline, American actor
- October 25 – Glenn Tipton, English rock guitarist
- October 26
  - Hillary Clinton, American politician, First Lady of the United States, Senator from New York, Secretary of State
  - Trevor Joyce, Irish poet
- October 29 – Richard Dreyfuss, American actor
- October 30 – Timothy B. Schmit, American musician
- October 31 – Herman Van Rompuy, Belgian politician

November

Joe Mantegna

- November 5 – Rubén Juárez, Argentine bandoneonist and singer-songwriter of tango (d. 2010)
- November 6
  - Jim Rosenthal, ITV sport presenter

- E. Lee Spence, pioneer underwater archaeologist and treasure hunter
- November 7
  - Yutaka Fukumoto, Japanese professional baseball player
  - Sondhi Limthongkul, Thai journalist, writer and founder of *Manager Daily*
- November 8
  - Minnie Riperton, American R&B singer (Lovin' You) (d. 1979)
  - Cassandra B. Whyte, American educator and higher education administrator
  - Lewis Yocum, American orthopedic surgeon (d. 2013)
- November 9 – Phil Driscoll, American Christian musician and trumpet player
- November 10 – Glen Buxton, American rock guitarist (d. 1997)
- November 13 – Joe Mantegna, American actor
- November 14 – P. J. O'Rourke, American journalist and satirist
- November 15 – Steven G. Kellman, American author and critic
- November 17 – Inky Mark, Canadian politician
- November 19
  - Bob Boone, American baseball player and manager
  - Anfinn Kallsberg, former Faroese Prime Minister
  - Lamar S. Smith, American politician
- November 20
  - Joe Walsh, American rock singer-songwriter, guitarist
  - Nurlan Balgimbayev, Kazakh politician (d. 2015)
- November 21

- Nickolas Grace, British actor
- Chua Ek Kay, Singaporean painter (d. 2008)
- November 23 – Alphons Orie, Dutch criminal lawyer and judge
- November 24
  - Mike Gorman, American sports announcer (Boston Celtics)
  - Dwight Schultz, American actor (*The A-Team*)
- November 25 – John Larroquette, American actor
- November 27 – Ismaïl Omar Guelleh, President of Djibouti
- November 29 – Mirza Khazar, Azerbaijani author
- November 30
  - Sergio Badilla Castillo, Chilean poet
  - Stuart Baird, English film editor, producer and director
  - Jude Ciccolella, American actor
  - Véronique Le Flaguais, Canadian actress
  - David Mamet, American playwright

December

Dilma Rousseff

- December 1 – Bob Fulton, English-born Australian rugby league player
- December 2 – Isaac Bitton, French rock band drummer
- December 7

- Johnny Bench, American baseball player
- Wendy Padbury, British actress
- December 8
    - Gregg Allman, American singer and songwriter
    - Gérard Blanc, French singer
    - Thomas R. Cech, American chemist, Nobel Prize laureate
- December 9 – Tom Daschle, U.S. Senator
- December 10 – Rainer Seifert, German field hockey player
- December 12 – Will Alsop, English architect
- December 14
    - Christopher Parkening, American guitarist
    - Dilma Rousseff, 36th President of Brazil
- December 16
    - Ben Cross, English actor
    - Vincent Matthews, American athlete
- December 18 – Leonid Yuzefovich, Russian crime fiction writer
- December 21
    - Bryan Hamilton, Irish footballer and football manager
    - Paco de Lucía, Spanish guitarist
- December 22
    - Mitsuo Tsukahara, Japanese gymnast
    - Porfirio Lobo, President of Honduras
- December 26 – Carlton Fisk, American baseball player
- December 28 – Aurelio Rodríguez, Mexican Major League Baseball player (d. 2000)
- December 29 – Ted Danson, American actor (*Cheers*)
- December 30 – Jeff Lynne, British musician
- December 31
    - Burton Cummings, Canadian rock musician

    - Tim Matheson, American actor, film director and producer

Date unknown

- Jean-François Batellier, French political cartoonist
- Peter Irniq, Commissioner of Nunavut
- Stephen LaBerge, Lucid dream researcher
- Jamie Donnelly, American film and stage actress

Deaths

January

Al Capone

- January 3 – Al Herpin (*The Man Who Never Slept*), notable insomniac (b. 1853)
- January 9
    - Herman Bing, German actor (b. 1889)
    - Karl Mannheim, Hungarian sociologist (b. 1893)
- January 10 – Arthur E. Andersen, American accountant (b. 1885)
- January 12 – Zdenko Blažeković, Croatian politician (b. 1915)
- January 14 – Bill Hewitt, American football player (Chicago Bears) and a member of the Pro Football Hall of Fame (b. 1909)

- January 15 – Elizabeth Short (*The Black Dahlia*), famous murder victim (b. 1924)
- January 19 – Manuel Machado Spanish poet (b. 1874)
- January 20
    - Andrew Volstead, American politician (b. 1860)
    - Josh Gibson, African-American baseball player and a member of the MLB Hall of Fame (b. 1911)
- January 22 – Vivienne Haigh-Wood Eliot, English writer (b. 1888)
- January 23
    - Pierre Bonnard, French painter (b. 1867)
- Roy Geiger, American general (b. 1885)
- January 25 – Al Capone, American gangster (b. 1899)
- January 26
    - Grace Moore, American opera singer (b. 1898)
    - Prince Gustaf Adolf, Duke of Västerbotten, Swedish prince (b. 1906)
- January 27 – Vassily Balabanov, administrator and Provincial Governor of Imperial Russia (b.1873)
- January 30 – Frederick Blackman, British plant physiologist (b.1866)

February

- February 3 – Petar Zivkovic, Serbian politician, former Prime Minister of Yugoslavia (b. 1879)
- February 6
    - O. Max Gardner, Governor of North Carolina (b. 1882)
    - Luigi Russolo, Italian Futurist painter and composer (b. 1885)
- February 11 – Martin Klein, Estonian wrestler (b.1884)
- February 12

- ○ Kurt Lewin, German-American psychologist (b. 1890)
- ○ Sidney Toler, American actor (b. 1874)
- February 27 – Heinrich Häberlin, Swiss Federal Councilor (b. 1868)

March

- March 5 – Alfredo Casella, Italian composer (b. 1883)
- March 10 – Harukichi Hyakutake, Japanese general (b. 1888)
- March 11 – Victor Lustig, Austrian-born con artist (b. 1890)
- March 12 – Walter Samuel Goodland, Governor of Wisconsin (b. 1862)
- March 18 – William C. Durant, American automobile pioneer (b. 1861)
- March 19 – Prudence Heward, Canadian painter (b. 1896)
- March 20 – Victor Goldschmidt, Swiss geochemist (b. 1888)
- March 21 – Homer Lusk Collyer, American hermit brother (*Collyer brothers*) (b. 1881)
- March 23 – Archduchess Louise of Austria, Princess of Tuscany (b. 1870)
- March 25 – Chen Cheng-po, Taiwanese painter (b. 1895)
- March 28
  - ○ Johnny Evers, American baseball player (Chicago Cubs) and a member of the MLB Hall of Fame (b. 1881)
  - ○ Karol Świerczewski, Polish military leader (b. 1897)
- March 30 – Arthur Machen, Welsh-born author (b. 1863)

April

George II of Greece

Henry Ford

Christian X of Denmark

- April 1 – King George II of Greece (b. 1890)
- April 7 – Henry Ford, American industrialist and automobile manufacturer (b. 1863)
- April 8 – Langley Collyer, American hermit brother (b. 1885)
- April 10 – John Ince, American actor (b. 1878)
- April 16 – Rudolf Höss, German commandant of Auschwitz concentration camp (executed) (b. 1900)

- April 20 – King Christian X of Denmark (b. 1870)
- April 24 – Willa Siebert Cather, American novelist (b. 1873)

May

- May 8 – Harry Gordon Selfridge, American department store magnate (b. 1858)
- May 13 – Sukanta Bhattacharya, Bengali poet (b. 1926)
- May 14 – John R. Sinnock, eighth Chief Engraver of the United States Mint (b. 1888)
- May 16 – Frederick Hopkins, English biochemist, recipient of the Nobel Prize in Physiology or Medicine (b. 1861)
- May 17 – George Forbes, 22nd Prime Minister of New Zealand (b. 1869)
- May 18 – Lucile Gleason, American actress (b. 1888)
- May 20 – Philipp Lenard, Austrian physicist, Nobel Prize laureate (b. 1862)
- May 23 – Seabiscuit, Thoroughbred Racehorse (b. 1933)
- May 24 – C. F. Ramuz, Swiss writer (b. 1878)
- May 28 – August Eigruber, Nazi war criminal (executed) (b. 1907)
- May 29 – Martin Gottfried Weiss, Nazi war criminal (executed) (b. 1905)
- May 30 – Georg Ludwig von Trapp, Austrian sailor, patriarch of the Von Trapp Family of *The Sound of Music* fame (b. 1880)
- May 31 – Adrienne Ames, American actress (b. 1907)

June

- June 6 – Władysław Raczkiewicz, former President of Poland (b. 1885)

- June 9 – J. Warren Kerrigan, American actor (b. 1879)
- June 11 – Richard Hönigswald, Hungarian-born American philosopher (b. 1875)
- June 17 – Maxwell Perkins, American literary editor (b. 1884)
- June 18 – Shigematsu Sakaibara, Japanese rear admiral and convicted war criminal (executed) (b. 1898)
- June 19 – Kōsō Abe, Japanese admiral (b. 1892)
- June 20 – Bugsy Siegel, American gangster (b. 1906)
- June 22 – Jim Tully, vagabond, pugilist, noted American writer (b. 1891)
- June 26 – Richard Bedford Bennett, 11th Prime Minister of Canada (b. 1870)

July

- July 12 – Jimmie Lunceford, American jazz musician (b. 1902)
- July 15 – Brandon Hurst, American stage and screen veteran (b. 1866)
- July 15 – Walter Donaldson, American songwriter (b. 1893)
- July 17 – Raoul Wallenberg, Swedish diplomat and humanitarian (presumed dead on this date) (b. 1912)
- July 19 – Aung San, Burmese nationalist (assassinated) (b. 1915)
- July 27 – Ivan Regen, Slovenian biologist (b. 1868)
- July 29
    - Leo Stein, American art collector and critic (b. 1872)
    - George Bausewine American baseball player and umpire (b. 1869)
- July 30 – Joseph Cook, 6th Prime Minister of Australia (b. 1860)

August

- August 3 – Vic Willis, American baseball player (Boston Braves) and a member of the MLB Hall of Fame (b. 1876)
- August 8 – Anton Ivanovich Denikin, Russian military leader (b. 1872)
- August 25 – Franz Cumont, Belgian archaeologist and historian (b. 1868)
- August 29
    - Manolete, Spanish bullfighter (gored) (b. 1917)
    - Kōtarō Nakamura, General of the Imperial Japanese Army (b. 1881)

September

- September 1 – Frederick Russell Burnham, American Scout, father of the international Scouting movement (b. 1861)
- September 8 – Victor Horta, Belgian Art Nouveau architect (b. 1861)
- September 9 – Ananda Coomaraswamy, philosopher (b. 1877)
- September 10 – Hatazō Adachi, Japanese general (suicide) (b. 1890)
- September 20
    - Fiorello H. La Guardia, Mayor of New York (b. 1882)
    - Jantina Tammes, Dutch plant biologist (b. 1871)
- September 21 – Harry Carey, American film actor (b. 1878)
- September 26 – Hugh Lofting, British-born writer (b. 1886)

October

Max Planck

- October 1 – Olive Borden, American actress (b. 1906)
- October 2 – P. D. Ouspensky, Russian mathematician (b. 1878)
- October 3 – Ernest L. Riebau, American politician (1895)
- October 4 – Max Planck, German physicist, Nobel Prize laureate (b. 1858)
- October 6 – Leevi Madetoja, Finnish composer (b. 1887)
- October 12 – Ian Standish Monteith Hamilton, British general (b. 1853)
- October 13 – Sidney Webb, English economist and social reformer (b. 1859)
- October 17 – John Halliday, American actor (b. 1880)
- October 23 – Carl Shelton, Gangster (b. 1888)
- October 24 – Dudley Digges, Irish actor (b. 1879)
- October 28 – Earl Snell, Governor of Oregon (plane crash) (b. 1895)
- October 29 – Frances Cleveland, American First Lady; wife of President Grover Cleveland (b. 1864)

November

Ernst Lubitsch

- November 1 – Man o' War, champion thoroughbred racehorse (b. 1917)
- November 8 – Mariano Benlliure, Spanish sculptor (b. 1862)
- November 15 – Eduard Ritter von Schleich, German fighter ace and air force general (b. 1888)
- November 20 – Georg Kolbe, German sculptor (b. 1877)
- November 25 – Léon-Paul Fargue, French writer (b. 1876)
- November 28
    - W. E. Lawrence, American silent film actor (b. 1896)
    - Philippe Leclerc de Hauteclocque, French general (b. 1902)
- November 30 – Ernst Lubitsch, German film director (b. 1892)

December

Stanley Baldwin

Victor Emmanuel III of Italy

- December 1
    - Aleister Crowley, British occultist (b. 1875)
    - G. H. Hardy, British mathematician (b. 1877)
- December 7
    - Tristan Bernard, French writer and lawyer (b. 1866)
    - Nicholas M. Butler, American president of Columbia University, recipient of the Nobel Peace Prize (b. 1862)
- December 13 – Nicholas Roerich, Russian painter (b. 1874)
- December 14
    - Stanley Baldwin, English Conservative politician, former Prime Minister of the United Kingdom (b. 1867)
    - Edward Higgins, General of The Salvation Army (b. 1864)
- December 15 – Arthur Machen, Welsh writer (b. 1863)
- December 17 – J. N. Brønsted, Danish chemist (b. 1879)
- December 25 – Gaspar G. Bacon, Lieutenant Governor of Massachusetts (b. 1886)
- December 27 – Johannes Winkler, German rocket pioneer (b. 1897)
- December 28 – Victor Emmanuel III of Italy (b. 1869)
- December 29 – Han van Meegeren, Dutch painter and forger (b. 1889)

- December 30 – Alfred North Whitehead, English mathematician and philosopher (b. 1861)

Nobel Prizes

- Physics – Edward Victor Appleton
- Chemistry – Sir Robert Robinson
- Medicine – Carl Ferdinand Cori, Gerty Cori, Bernardo Houssay
- Literature – André Gide
- Peace – The Friends Service Council (UK) and The American Friends Service Committee (USA), on behalf of the Religious Society of Friends

In the News

CIA established in 1947.

UFO allegedly found on July 7th in the Roswell UFO incident.

A research team at Bell Laboratories invents the transistor.

Ammonium nitrate cargo of SS Grandcap explodes in Texas City, Texas - 552 dead, 3000 injured.

The classic holiday film "Miracle on 34th Street" premieres.

First Of The Dead Sea Scrolls Found in caves near Wadi Qumran.

Her Royal Highness Princess Elizabeth marries the Duke of Edinburgh at Westminster Abbey, London.

The coldest temp in North America (−63 °C)is recorded at Snag, Yukon, Canada.

Popular Films - Miracle on 34th Street, Road to Rio, The Jolson Story.

The Diary of Anne Frank is published.

Made in the USA
Middletown, DE
14 September 2019